BELLA
and the
UMBRELLA

Written by Pearl Atkins Schwartz   Pictures by Chris Lensch

First published by Experience Early Learning Company
7243 Scotchwood Lane, Grawn, Michigan 49637 USA

Text Copyright ©2016 by Experience Early Learning Co.
Printed and Bound in the USA

ISBN: 978-1-937954-37-6
visit us at www.ExperienceEarlyLearning.com

Bella and her mother collected many different doohickeys for the kitchen.

2

So she wasn't surprised when on a cloudy Saturday morning, her mother said, "Let's go to Fancy Finds today. Maybe we can find something new, something interesting, something useful."

4

In the shop on Grafton Street, they went to the rear of the store where the kitchen gadgets were kept. Bella followed her mother, passing the racks of men's and ladies' clothing, lamps and teacups, and old cookbooks.

squeak!

Cook Book

CULINARY INSTITUTE COOKBOOK

5

Bella watched her mother examine a rusty ice-cream maker, a food-chopping tool, and a box camera with the lens missing. There was a green Mixmaster with only one mixing wand, a squeaky nutcracker, and a coffee pot with a crack on its side.

6

It wasn't long before they decided this was not a good day to shop at Fancy Finds. On their way out, Bella's mother came to a sudden stop near the door. Poking out of a pot was a bright pink umbrella with an orange ruffle. She lifted it out and felt the fabric with her thumb and forefinger.

"Mmm," she said. "It feels like silk." She opened the umbrella, examined the spokes, and found the price tag. She took it to the cash register and paid for it. A few minutes later, they left the Fancy Finds store, the umbrella tucked under her mother's arm.

Monday was an off-and-on rainy day. The school bus waited down the street on the corner. Bella put on her yellow slicker. The rain went plunk, plunk on the windows.

"Mom," Bella wailed. "I can't find my blue umbrella!" Bella and her mother looked in her closet and behind the door. They found a penny and a broken crayon.

They looked behind the curtain and under the bed. All they found was half of a dust-covered peanut butter sandwich and a smelly red sock.

Bella looked out the window. Her friends were rushing down the street to the bus. "The bus will leave without me," Bella said. "Where is my umbrella?" This time she tried her mother's closet. On the shelf was the new pink and orange umbrella, with its tag still attached.

"Mom, there's the umbrella you bought at Fancy Finds," Bella said with a touch of hope in her voice.

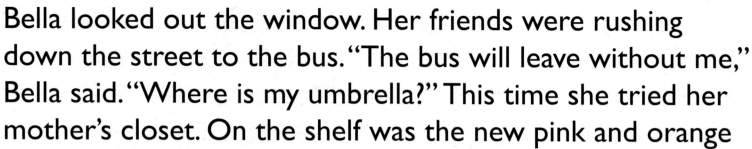

"**No way**," her mother said.
"You might lose it."

"Honk, honk," the school bus blasted.

"Oh, **please, please** let me use your umbrella!" Bella hopped from one foot to the other.
"I won't lose it. I promise!"

Bella's mother reached up to the closet shelf and handed her the umbrella.

Bella ran down the street holding the pink and orange umbrella over her head.

"DON'T LOSE THE UMBRELLA!" her mother called.

16

Out of breath, Bella climbed into the bus.
"Hi, Charley," she said to the driver.

"Whoa! Fancy umbrella!" a boy hooted.

She took the last place on the bus and laid the dripping umbrella on the floor under her seat. The bus took off with the rain going plunkety-plunk on the window.

When they arrived at school, Bella dashed out of the bus with her friends.

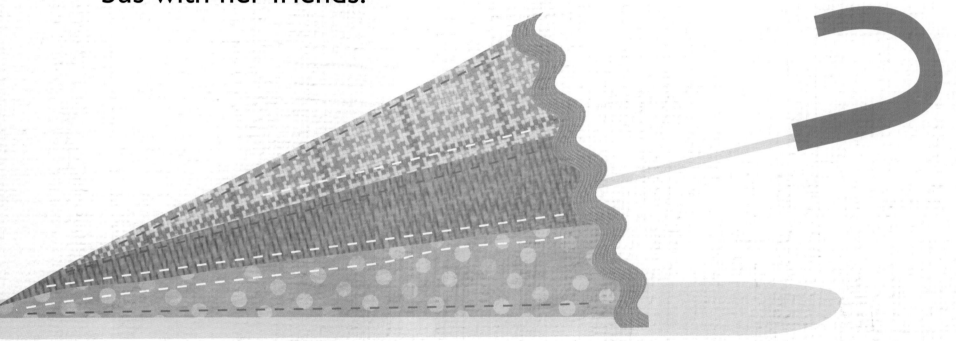

But she forgot the umbrella.

When his bus was empty, Charley started to drive back to the bus garage. On the way, he passed the fruit market where a mound of apples sat on a stand under an awning. Those apples looked mighty good to Charley. He decided to get one for his lunch.

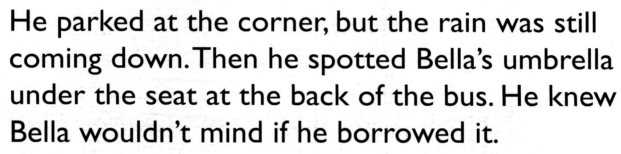

He parked at the corner, but the rain was still coming down. Then he spotted Bella's umbrella under the seat at the back of the bus. He knew Bella wouldn't mind if he borrowed it.

As soon as he reached the awning, he closed the umbrella and tucked it under his arm. He picked out an apple, and just as he lifted it off the top, the mound of fruit started to roll helter-skelter down the street.

23

Charlie dropped the umbrella on the ground as he tried to grab the apples. The owner of the store ran out, and he and Charlie chased the apples.

Charlie was a bit flustered from all the excitement. He paid for his apple, went back to his bus, and drove away.

But he forgot the umbrella.

In the meantime, Buddy, a neighborhood dog, had been watching all the action.

When he saw the umbrella drop to the ground, he picked it up between his teeth and pranced down the street, wagging his tail.

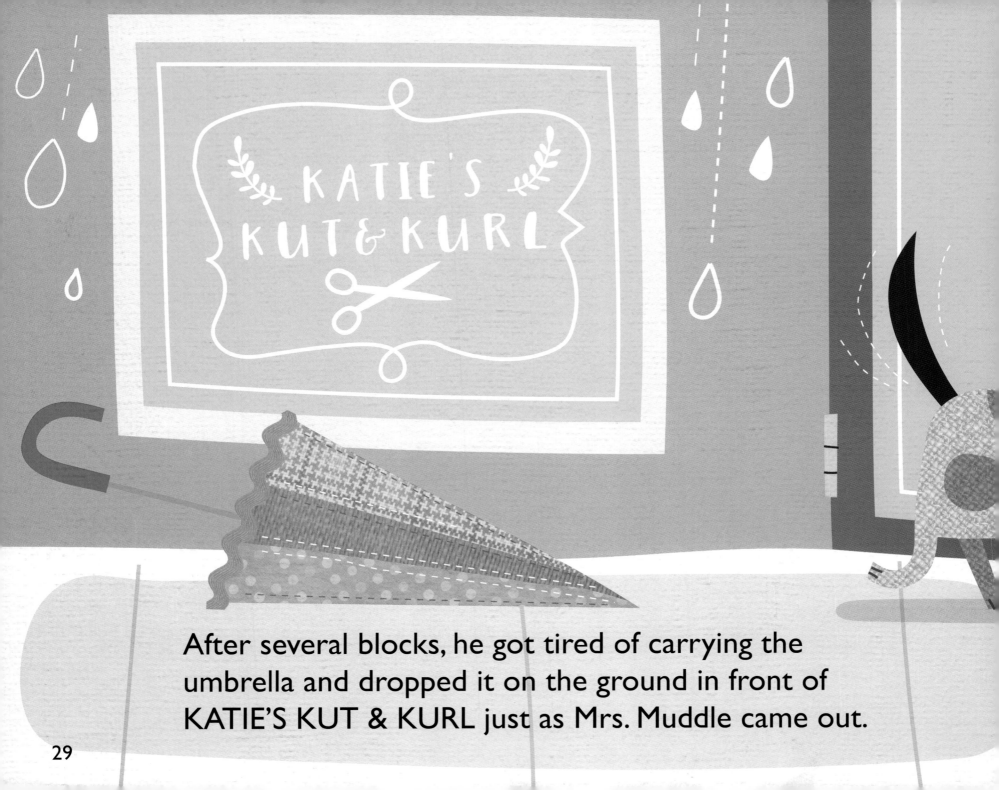

After several blocks, he got tired of carrying the umbrella and dropped it on the ground in front of KATIE'S KUT & KURL just as Mrs. Muddle came out.

Mrs. Muddle stood in the doorway and saw the raindrops falling down. "Oh, no," she said. "My new hairdo will be ruined!"

Then she noticed an umbrella lying on the ground near the door. She picked it up and went on her way to the supermarket to buy cereal.

In the store, Mrs. Muddle walked up and down the cereal aisle. She wondered which one she should buy.

Snoopy Loops

mg Time

New!

Snappy *Pops

TrickyKix

She leaned the umbrella against a shelf and picked up a box of Snappy Pops. She put it back and pulled out a box of Snoopy Loops. She put that back. Tricky Kix looked good, but Mrs. Muddle could not make up her mind. So she decided not to buy any cereal. Mrs. Muddle left the supermarket to go home.

But she forgot the umbrella.

The grocery clerk, Timmy, was sweeping the floor when he saw an umbrella leaning against a shelf. He looked around. Nobody seemed to be searching for anything so he put the umbrella in the "Lost and Found" box at the back of the store.

Then he went to help deliver grocery orders.
The name Minelli was written on the first box.

When Timmy loaded the basket on the back of his bicycle, he felt a rain drop on his head. "Here comes the rain again," he said. So he borrowed the umbrella in the "Lost and Found" box.

He rode his bicycle steering with one hand and holding the umbrella over his head with the other hand.

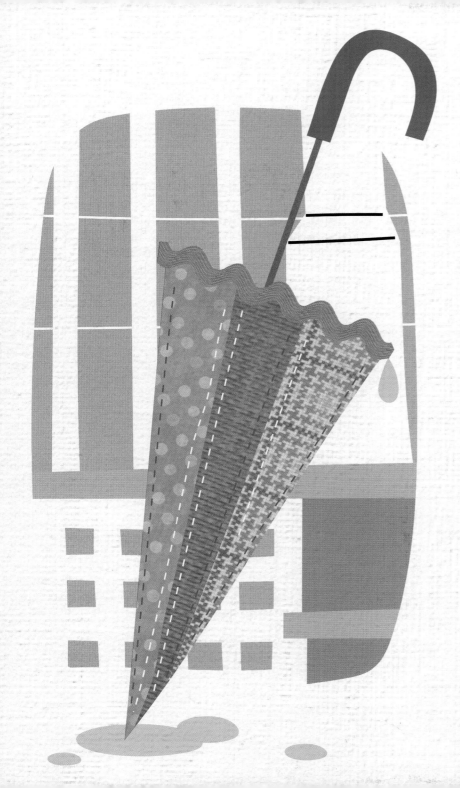

By the time he arrived at the Minelli house, the rain had stopped. He placed the umbrella on the porch and rang the doorbell. Bella's mother took the carton of groceries, and Timmy got on his bike and rode away.

But he forgot the umbrella.

In her math class at school Bella glanced out the window at the rain and remembered the umbrella. She didn't have it. Her heart sank. She couldn't concentrate on what her teacher was saying.

"If you have a dozen oranges," Mrs. Smart said, "and you give four of them away, how many will you have left? Bella?"

"Eight umbrellas," Bella replied. "OOPS...I mean eight oranges."

At three o'clock, Bella walked home from school. The rain had stopped, and the sun was shining, but she was worried. She remembered her mother's words that morning:

"DON'T LOSE THE UMBRELLA!"

What was she going to say?

44

As she came near the porch, she slowed down. Her heart jumped. Leaning against the porch railing was the pink umbrella with an orange ruffle.

She leaped up the steps and grabbed it just as her mother opened the door to greet her.

"Hi, Mom. Here's your umbrella, safe and sound."

46

Bella went right upstairs to her room.
She had something to think about.

The End

47